PIANO · VOCAL · GUITAR

SUPERTRAMP
GREATEST HITS

CONTENTS

2   AIN'T NOBODY BUT ME

10   BLOODY WELL RIGHT

14   BREAKFAST IN AMERICA

18   CANNONBALL

26   CRIME OF THE CENTURY

31   DREAMER

42   FROM NOW ON

50   GIVE A LITTLE BIT

55   GOODBYE STRANGER

62   IT'S RAINING AGAIN

67   THE LOGICAL SONG

72   MY KIND OF LADY

80   RUDY

92   TAKE THE LONG WAY HOME

ISBN 978-0-634-04193-8

HAL·LEONARD®
CORPORATION
7777 W. BLUEMOUND RD. P.O. BOX 13819 MILWAUKEE, WI 53213

Visit Hal Leonard Online at
www.halleonard.com

AIN'T NOBODY BUT ME

Words and Music by RICK DAVIES
and ROGER HODGSON

Slow and Bluesy

Let me tell you a sto-ry that-'ll make a change;

there's no one 'neath the stars a - bove.

Well, you can run, you know he'll find you.
You see, I got an ug - ly dis - po - si - tion;

It don't mat - ter now, just look be - hind you.
some - times I'm mean, some - times I'm vi - cious.

You had the warn - ing; you knew the score.
I'm Doc - tor Je - kyll and Mis - ter Hyde.

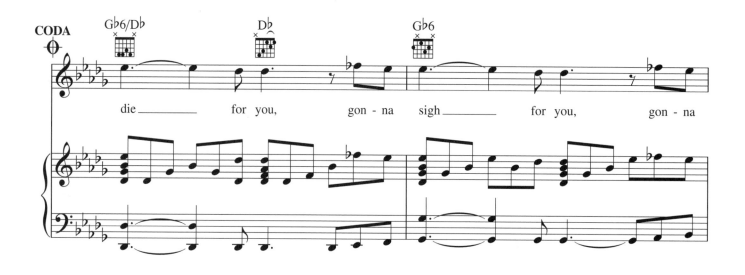

die _____ for you, gon - na sigh _____ for you, gon - na

try _____ for you, gon - na lie _____ for you, gon - na die _____ for you.

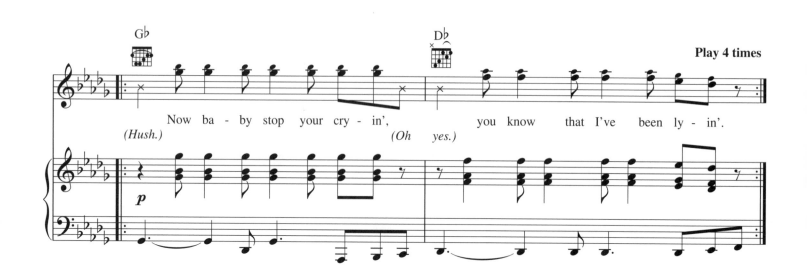

Now ba - by stop your cry - in', you know that I've been ly - in'.
(Hush.) (Oh yes.)

p

Play 4 times

Now ba - by stop your cry - in,' ah.

(Hush.)

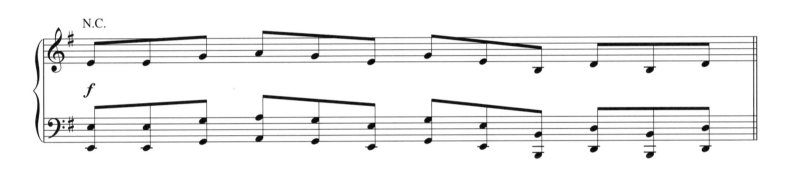

Repeat and Fade

Optional Ending

BLOODY WELL RIGHT

Words and Music by RICK DAVIES
and ROGER HODGSON

So, you think __ your school - ing's __ pho - ney;
Write your prob - lems down in ___ de - tail;

BREAKFAST IN AMERICA

Words and Music by RICK DAVIES
and ROGER HODGSON

Moderate Rock

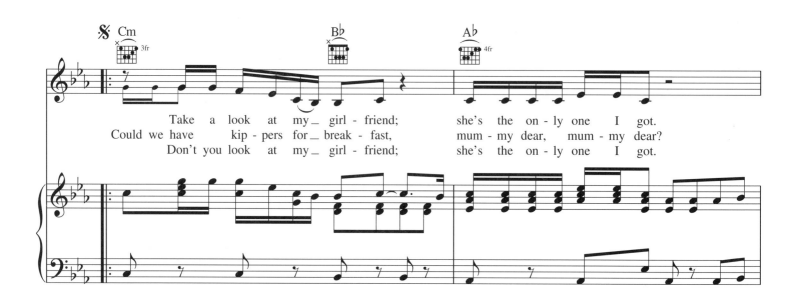

Take a look at my_ girl - friend; she's the on - ly one I got.
Could we have kip - pers for_ break - fast, mum - my dear, mum - my dear?
Don't you look at my_ girl - friend; she's the on - ly one I got.

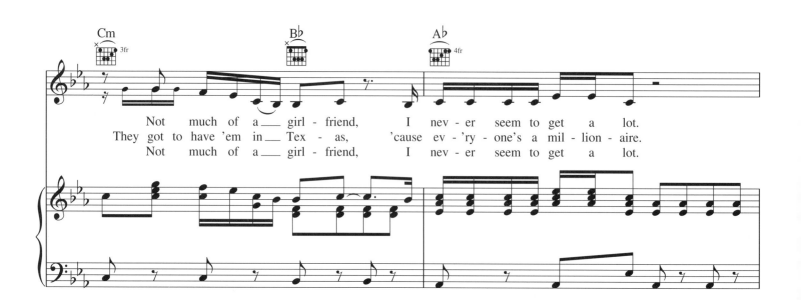

Not much of a_ girl - friend, I nev - er seem to get a lot.
They got to have 'em in_ Tex - as, 'cause ev - 'ry - one's a mil - lion - aire.
Not much of a_ girl - friend, I nev - er seem to get a lot.

Take a jum - bo 'cross the wa - ter, like to see A - mer - i - ca,
I'm a win - ner, I'm a sin - ner. Do you want my au - to - graph?
Take a jum - bo 'cross the wa - ter, like to see A - mer - i - ca,

see the girls in Cal - i - for - nia. I'm hop - ing it's going to come true, but there's
I'm a los - er, what a jok - er. I'm play - ing my jokes up - on you while there's
see the girls in Cal - i - for - nia. I'm hop - ing it's go - ing to come true, but there's

not a lot___ I can do.
noth - ing bet - ter to do.
not a lot___ I can do.

CANNONBALL

Words and Music by
RICK DAVIES

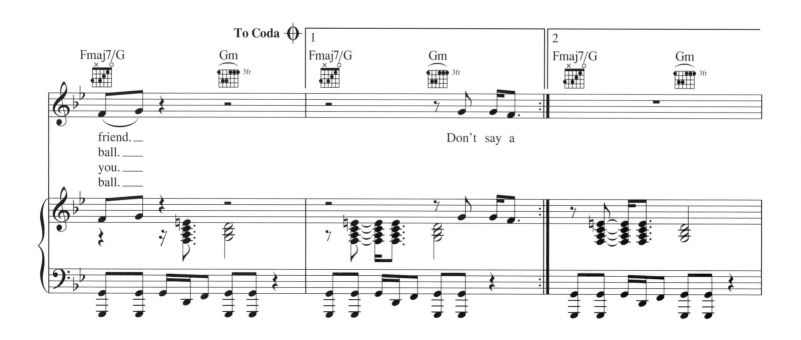

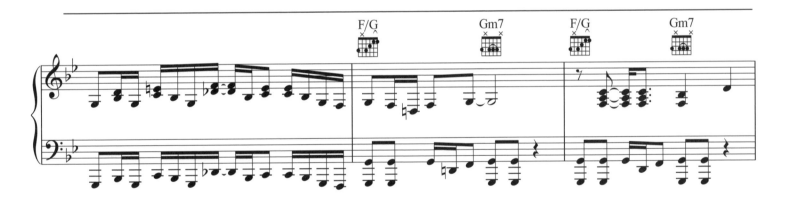

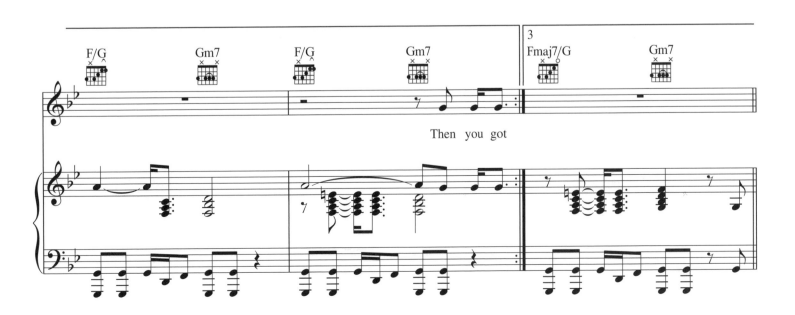

Then you got

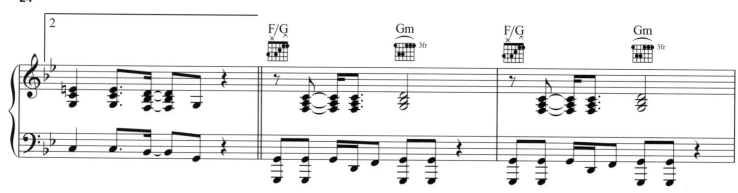

F/G   Gm   F/G   Gm

D.S. al Coda

O - kay, that's

CODA Fmaj7/G   Gm

Spoken: Like a cannonball!

E♭/G   Gm6   E♭/G

CRIME OF THE CENTURY

Words and Music by RICK DAVIES
and ROGER HODGSON

Now they're plan-ning the crime of the cen-tu-ry.

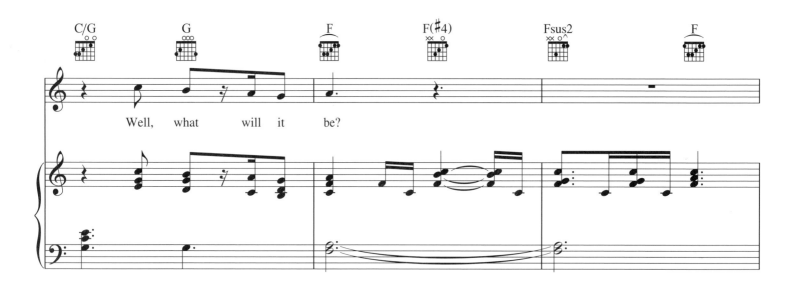

Well, what will it be?

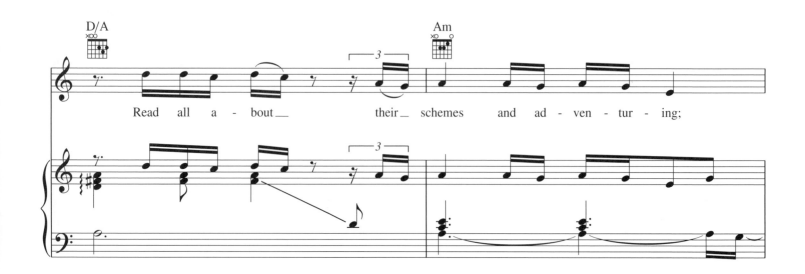

Read all a-bout their schemes and ad-ven-tur-ing;

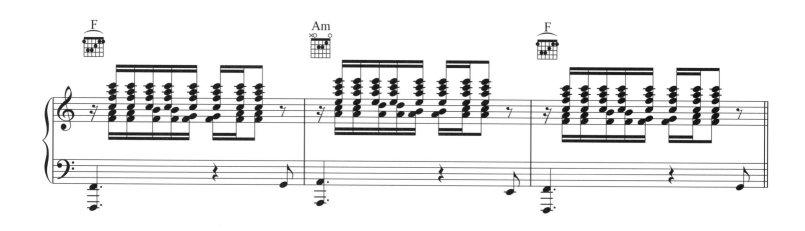

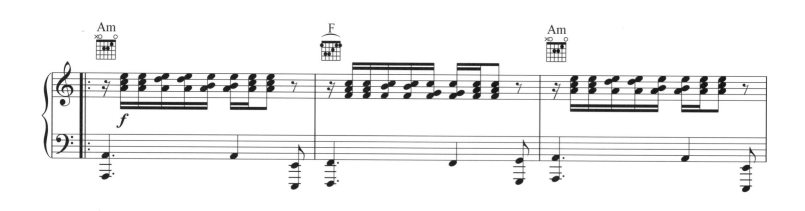

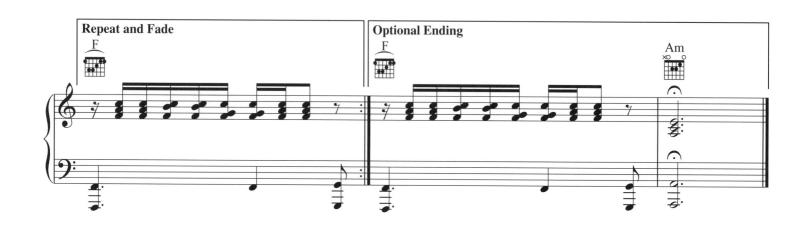

DREAMER

Words and Music by RICK DAVIES
and ROGER HODGSON

36

Can you put your hands in your head, oh no!   Oh

no!

Optional Ending

rit.

Fade out

FROM NOW ON

Words and Music by RICK DAVIES
and ROGER HODGSON

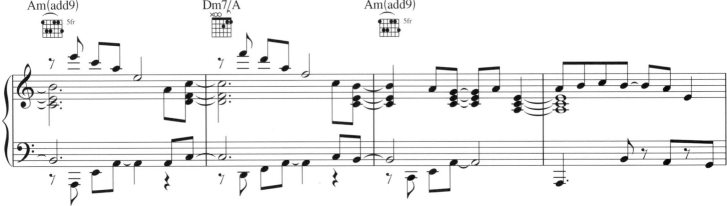

GIVE A LITTLE BIT

Words and Music by RICK DAVIES
and ROGER HODGSON

Give a lit-tle bit, give a lit-tle bit of your love to me. I'll give a lit-tle bit, I'll give a lit-tle bit of my { love / life

54

GOODBYE STRANGER

Words and Music by RICK DAVIES
and ROGER HODGSON

Moderate Rock

It was an ear - ly morn - ing yes - ter - day,
I be - lieve in what you say
some they do and some they don't,

I was up be - fore the dawn.
is the un - dis - pu - ted truth.
and some you just can't tell.

And I
But I
And

56

real - ly have ___ en - joyed my stay, ___
have to have ___ things my own way ___
some they will ___ and some they won't.

but I must be mov - in' on. ___ Like a
just to keep me in ___ my youth. ___ Like a
With some it's ___ just ___ as well. ___ You can

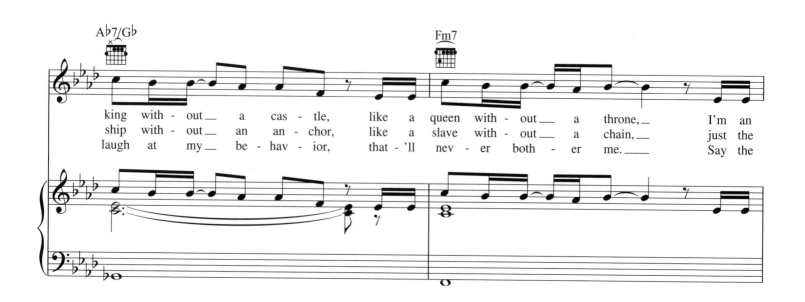

king with - out ___ a cas - tle, like a queen with - out ___ a throne, ___ I'm an
ship with - out ___ an an - chor, like a slave with - out ___ a chain, ___ just the
laugh at my ___ be - hav - ior, that 'll nev - er both - er me. ___ Say the

IT'S RAINING AGAIN

Words and Music by RICK DAVIES
and ROGER HODGSON

Moderately, with a steady beat

THE LOGICAL SONG

Words and Music by RICK DAVIES
and ROGER HODGSON

Moderate Rock

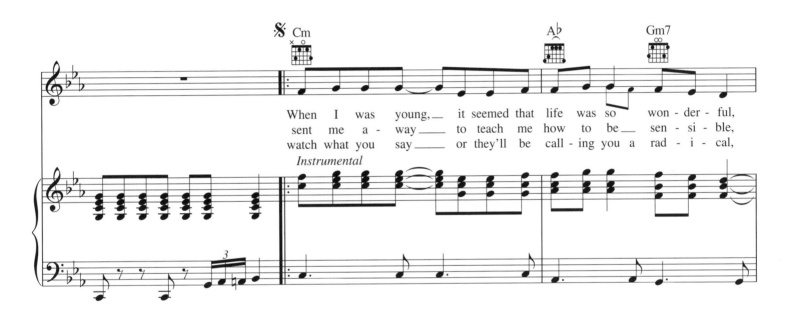

When I was young,___ it seemed that life was so won-der-ful,
sent me a-way___ to teach me how to be___ sen-si-ble,
watch what you say___ or they'll be call-ing you a rad-i-cal,

Instrumental

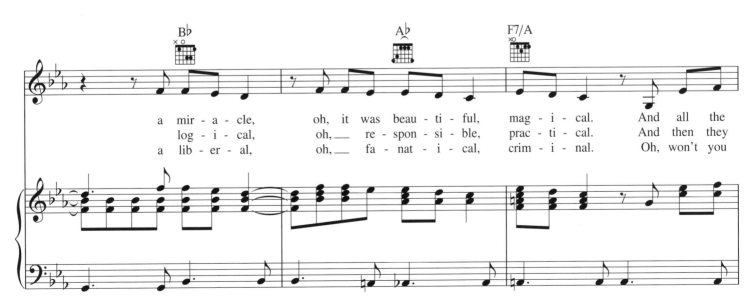

a mir-a-cle, oh, it was beau-ti-ful, mag-i-cal. And all the
log-i-cal, oh,___ re-spon-si-ble, prac-ti-cal. And then they
a lib-er-al, oh,___ fa-nat-i-cal, crim-i-nal. Oh, won't you

MY KIND OF LADY

Words and Music by RICK DAVIES
and ROGER HODGSON

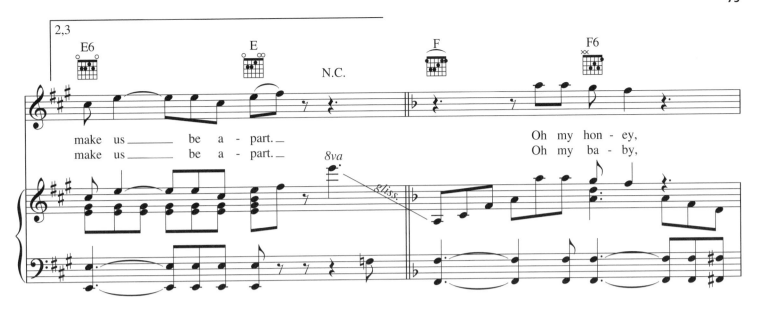

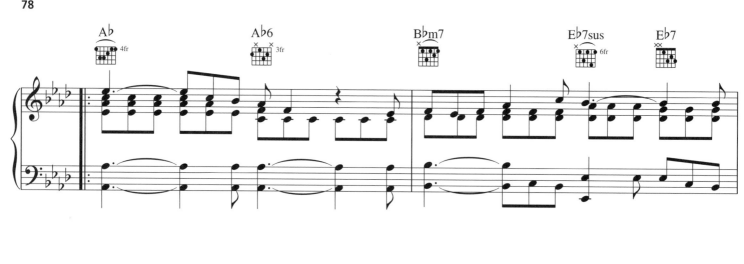

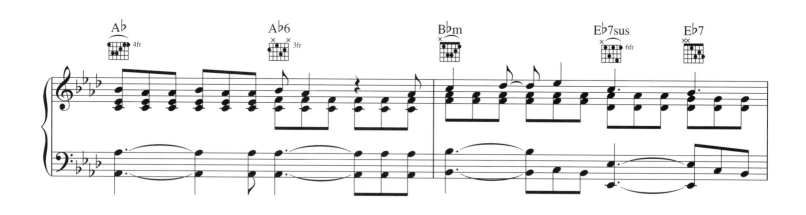

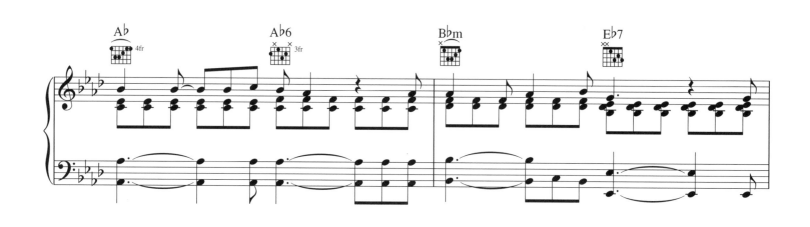

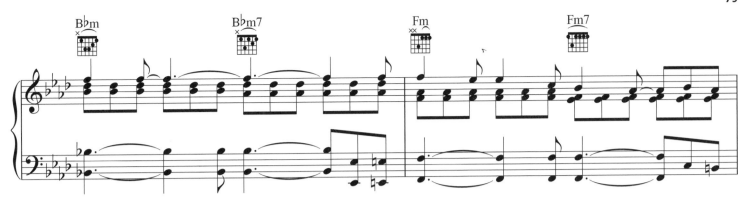

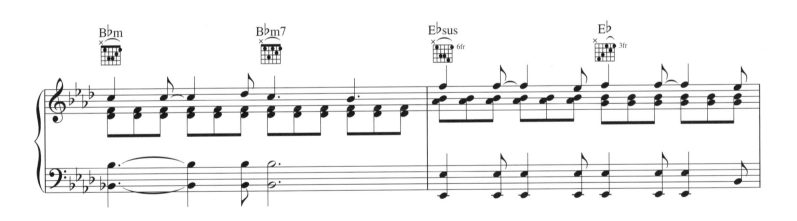

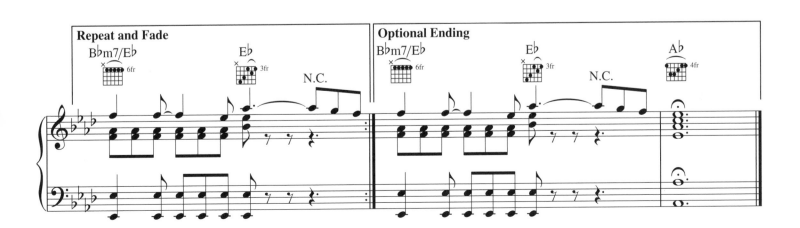

RUDY

Words and Music by RICK DAVIES
and ROGER HODGSON

Ru - dy's on a train to no - where,   half - way   down___
He ain't so - phis - ti - ca - ted   or well___

see

that __ it may come, but too late, ___

too late, too late.

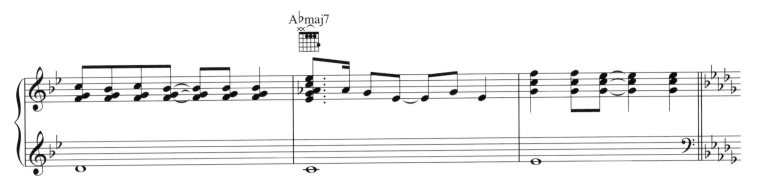

Instrumental Solo

Play 6 times

Solo ends   All

through   your   life, _____   all ____   through the
can   you   live _____   with - out   love, ____   it's   not

TAKE THE LONG WAY HOME

Words and Music by RICK DAVIES
and ROGER HODGSON

So you think you're a Ro-me-o _____ play-ing a part in a pic-ture show, well, take the
When lone-ly days turn to lone-ly nights _____ you take a trip to the cit-y lights, and take the

long way home, take the long way home.